WELSH FOR BEGINNERS

Angela Wilkes

Illustrated by John Shackell

Designed by Roger Priddy
Edited by Nicole Irving
Language Consultant: Tudur W. Evans

CONTENTS

About this book

Did you know that Welsh has been spoken for longer than any other language in Europe? This book shows you that learning Welsh is a lot easier than you might think. It teaches you the Welsh you will find useful in everyday situations.

You can find out how to . . .

talk about yourself

and your home,

count and tell the time,

say what you like,

find your way around

and ask for what you want in shops.

How you learn

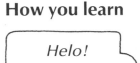

Picture strips like this show you what to say in each situation. Read the speech bubbles and see how much you can understand by

yourself, then look up any words you do not know. Words and phrases are repeated again and again, to help you remember them.

The book starts with really easy things to say and gets more difficult towards the end.

2

New words

All the new words you come across are listed on each double page, so you can look them up as you go along. If you forget any words you can look them up in the Glossary on pages 46-48. *If you see an asterisk by a word, it means that there is a note about it at the bottom of the page.

Grammar

Boxes like this around words show where new grammar is explained. You will find Welsh easier if you learn some of its grammar, but don't worry if you don't understand it all straight away. You can look up any of the grammar used in the book on pages 42-43.

How to say things

On page 7 you can find out about the Welsh alphabet. On page 11 you can find out how to pronounce the different letters in Welsh. On page 43 you can find out about Welsh words which change their first letters.

Puzzles

All the way through the book there are puzzles and quizzes to help you practise your Welsh and test yourself on what you have learnt. You can check whether your answers are right on pages 44-45.

Practising your Welsh

Write all the new words you learn in a notebook and try to learn a few every day. Keep going over them and you will soon remember them.

Ask a friend to keep testing you on your Welsh. Even better, ask someone to learn Welsh with you so that you can practise on each other.

Rydw i eisiau . . .

When you are in Wales try to speak as much Welsh as you can. Don't be afraid of making mistakes. No one will mind.

Saying "Hello"

The first thing you should know how to say in Welsh is "Hello". There are different greetings for different times of the day.

Try to learn the useful greetings in these pictures. The Pronunciation guide on page 41 will help you to say the words properly.

Saying "Hello"

Helo!

This is how you say "Hello" to your friends.

Bore da.

Bore da.

This is how you say "Good morning" to someone.

Noswaith dda.

This is how you say "Good evening" to someone.

Saying "Goodbye"

Hwyl.

Hwyl fawr.

Hwyl fawr.

Da boch.

Hwyl or **Hwyl fawr** means "Goodbye, have fun".

Da boch is another way of saying "Goodbye".

Saying "Goodnight"

Nos da.

You only say **Nos da** last thing at night.

How are you?

This is how to greet someone and ask how they are.

This person is saying that she is fine, thank you . . .

. . . but this person is saying things aren't too good.

Sut wyt ti?

This list shows you different ways of saying how you are. How do you think these people would answer if you asked them how they were?

yn dda iawn   very well
yn dda   well
yn weddol   fairly well
dim yn dda   not well
yn wael   poorly
yn ofnadwy   terrible

5

What is your name?

Here you can find out how to ask someone their name and tell them yours, and how to introduce your friends.

Read the picture strip and see how much you can understand. Then try doing the puzzles on the page opposite.

New words

beth?	what?
enw	name
enwau	names
beth ydy dy enw di?	what is your name?
Gareth ydw i	I am Gareth
fy enw i ydy	my name is
dyma	here is/this is
fy ffrind	my friend
ei enw o	his name
ei henw hi	her name
eu henwau nhw	their names
pwy?	who?
pwy ydy hon?	who is she?
pwy ydy o?	who is he?
dyna	that is

"His", "her" and "their"

In Welsh, you use **ei** to say either "his" or "her", e.g. **ei enw o** (his name), **ei henw hi** (her name), but notice how the word changes after **ei** depending on whether you mean "his" or "her". You can find more about this on page 42.

The word for "their" is **eu**, e.g. **eu henwau nhw** (their names).

> Helo, beth ydy dy enw di?

> Gareth ydw i.

> Fy enw i ydy Mair.

Introducing friends

> Dyma fy ffrind, ei enw o ydy Rhys.

> Pwy ydy hi?

> Dyma fy ffrind ei henw hi ydy Mari.

> Beth ydy eu henwau nhw?

> Eu henwau nhw ydy Ann a Gari.

6

What are they called?

Can you answer these questions in Welsh?

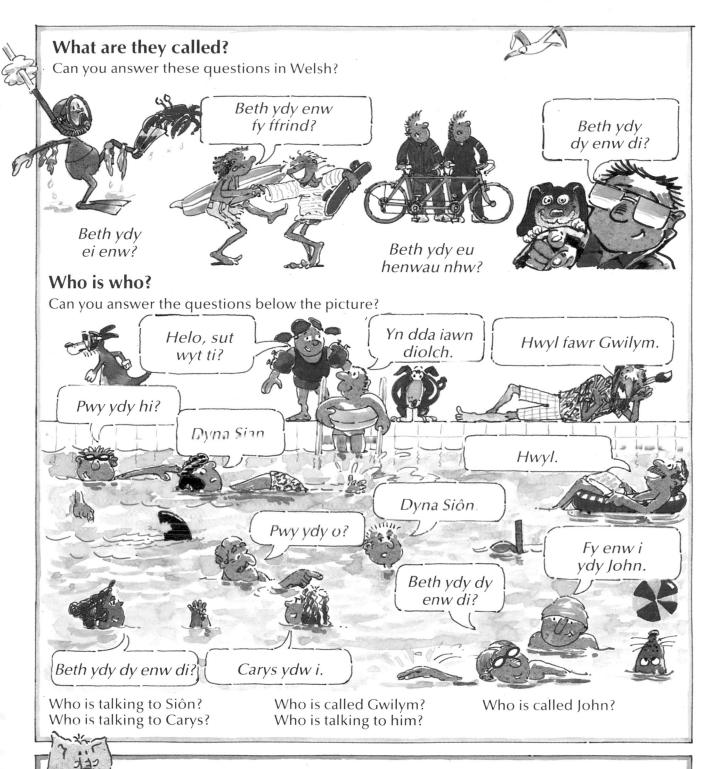

Who is who?

Can you answer the questions below the picture?

Who is talking to Siôn?
Who is talking to Carys?

Who is called Gwilym?
Who is talking to him?

Who is called John?

Points to remember

The Welsh alphabet is different from the English. It will help you to learn it now: A B C Ch D Dd E F Ff G Ng H I L Ll M N O P Ph R Rh S T Th U W Y. As you can see, the Welsh alphabet has no J, K, Q, V, X, or Z.* You can find out how to say Welsh letters on page 41.

*When Welsh uses English words you do find "J", e.g. **garej** (garage).

Finding out what things are called

Everything in this picture has its name on it. See if you can learn the names for everything, then try the memory test at the bottom of the opposite page. You can find out how to say "the" in Welsh at the bottom of this page.

Welsh nouns (naming words)

In Welsh the word for "the" is **y** or **yr** : **y** when the noun begins with a consonant, e.g. **y drws** (the door), and **yr** when the noun begins with a vowel, e.g. **yr aderyn** (the bird).

(Remember that in Welsh "w" and "y" are vowels.) There is no word for "a" or "an" in Welsh, you just use the noun on its own.

simne	chimney	**ffenestr**	window	**blodyn**	flower
coeden	tree	**tŷ***	house	**haul**	sun
aderyn	bird	**drws**	door	**nyth**	nest
cath	cat	**ffens**	fence	**garej**	garage
tô*	roof	**ci**	dog	**car**	car

*The circumflex or "little roof", e.g. in **tô**, is used above a vowel to make that vowel long.

Asking what things are called

Don't worry if you don't know what something is called in Welsh. To find out what it is, just ask someone **beth ydy hwn?** Look at the list of useful phrases below, then read the picture strip to see how to use them.

beth ydy hwn?	what is this?
hefyd	also
na	no
yn Gymraeg	in Welsh
yn Saesneg	in English
a**	and

Beth ydy hwn?

Blodyn. *

Blodyn ydy hwn hefyd?

Na, coeden.

Beth ydy hwn yn Gymraeg?

Drws.

A beth ydy hwn?

Ci!

A beth ydy hwn yn Saesneg?

A dog!

Can you remember?

Cover up the opposite page and see if you can name all of these things in Welsh. Try to say whether they are **y** or **yr** words.

*Remember there is no word for "a" or "an" in Welsh, so to say "a flower" you use the noun on its own: **blodyn.** **A** (and) changes to **ac** in front of words beginning with a vowel.

9

Where do you come from?

Here you can find out how to ask people where they come from. You can also find out how to ask if they speak Welsh.

New words

o*ble wyt ti'n dod?	where do you come from?
rydw i'n dod o . . .	I come from . . .
rydw i'n byw yn	I live in
o Loegr	from England
mae fy ffrind o Ffrainc	my friend is from France
wyt ti'n siarad?	do you speak?
dipyn bach	a little
Cymraeg	Welsh
Ffrangeg	French
Saesneg	English

Countries

Cymru	Wales
Lloegr	England
Yr Alban	Scotland
Yr Almaen	Germany
Ffrainc	France
Sbaen	Spain
Yr Eidal	Italy
Iwerddon	Ireland
Awstria	Austria
Rwsia	Russia

Where do you come from?

O ble wyt ti'n dod?

Rydw i'n dod o Gymru.

Ble wyt ti'n byw?

Rydw i'n byw yn Llandudno.

O ble wyt ti'n dod?

Rydw i'n dod o Loegr.

Mae fy ffrind o Ffrainc. Mae hi'n byw yn Paris.

Do you speak Welsh?

Wyt ti'n siarad Cymraeg?

Ydw, dipyn bach.

Wyt ti'n siarad Cymraeg Sian?

Ydw rydw i'n siarad Cymraeg a dipyn bach o Ffrangeg.

Mae Harri'n siarad Cymraeg, Saesneg a Ffrangeg.

*O means "from". There is another word o which means "he" or "him".

Who comes from where?

These are the contestants for an international dancing competition. They have come from all over the world. The compère does not speak any Welsh and does not understand where anyone comes from. Read about the contestants, then see if you can tell him what he wants to know. His questions are beneath the picture.

Mae Angus yn dod o'r Alban.

Mae Marie a Pierre yn dod o Ffrainc.

Mae Hari ac Indira yn dod o'r India.

Mae Yuri yn dod o Rwsia. Mae o'n byw yn Moscow.

Mae Franz yn dod o Awstria.

Dyma Lolita. Mae hi yn dod o Sbaen.

Where do they all come from?

Where does Franz come from?
What are the French contestants called?
Is Lolita Italian or Spanish?

Is there a Scottish contestant?
Where do Marie and Pierre come from?
Who lives in Moscow? Where is Moscow?

---

	bod	to be
Verbs (action words) The Welsh verb **bod**, "to be", is used to form other verbs: **rydw i** means "I am", and **rydw i yn siarad** means either "I talk" or "I am talking". The words for "I", "you" etc, are **i** (I), **ti** (you*), **O** (he), **hi** (she), **ni** (we), **chi** (you*) and **nhw** (they). Notice how, in Welsh, these words come after the verb.	**rydw i** **rwyt ti** **mae o** **mae hi** **rydyn ni** **rydych chi** **maen nhw**	I am you are he is she is we are you are they are

---

Points to remember

In Welsh, **yn** before a verb shows that the action is happening now. To say both "I talk" and "I am talking", you say **rydw i yn siarad**; "you talk/are talking" is **rwyt ti yn siarad**, and so on.

Yn is often shortened to **'n: rydw i'n siarad.** You also use **yn** before a describing word, e.g. **rydw i yn oer** (I am cold).

---

*"You" is **ti** when you are talking to a friend, but **chi** when you are talking to more than one person (plural) or to an adult (polite). See pages 23 and 30.

More about you

Here you can find out how to count up to 20, say how old you are and say how many brothers and sisters you have.

New words

faint ydy dy oed di?	how old are you?
rydw i yn naw oed	I am nine (years old)
oes gen ti?	have you (got)?
brawd	brother
chwaer	sister
oes gen ti frawd a chwaer?	have you got any brothers and sisters?
mae gen i	I have
eu hoed nhw	their ages
does gen i ddim	I haven't (got)
bron yn	nearly
ond	but

Numbers*

1	un
2	dau/dwy**
3	tri/tair**
4	pedwar/pedair**
5	pump
6	chwech
7	saith
8	wyth
9	naw
10	deg
11	undeg un
12	undeg dau
13	undeg tri
14	undeg pedwar
15	undeg pump
16	undeg chwech
17	undeg saith
18	undeg wyth
19	undeg naw
20	dauddeg

How old are you?

Have you got any brothers and sisters?

* You will find a complete list of numbers on page 40. **Dau, tri and pedwar change to dwy, tair and pedair when used with feminine nouns (see page 18).

How old are they?

Read what these children are saying, then see if you can say how old they all are.

> *Mae Griff yn undeg tri.*

> *Rydyn ni yn undeg pump.*

> *Mae Gwen yn undeg un.*

> *Mae Maldwyn bron yn undeg pedwar.*

> *Rydw i yn chwech. Mae Iwan yn naw.*

Maldwyn   Catrin a Rhian   Griff   Gwen   Iwan   Nerys

How many brothers and sisters?

Below you can read how many brothers and sisters the children have. Can you work out who has which brothers and sisters?

Mae gan* Catrin a Rhian un brawd a dwy chwaer.

Mae gan Gwen dair chwaer a dau frawd.

Mae gan Maldwyn bump chwaer ond dim brawd.

Mae gan Iwan un brawd ond dim chwaer.

Does gan Griff ddim brawd na chwaer, ond mae ganddo un ci.

How to say "I have" and "I haven't"

	to have
mae gen i	I have
mae gen ti	you have
mae ganddo	he has*
mae ganddi	she has*
mae gynnon ni	we have
mae gynnoch chi	you have (pl)
mae ganddyn nhw	they have*

	not to have
does gen i ddim	I haven't
does gen ti ddim	you haven't
does ganddo ddim	he hasn't
does ganddi ddim	she hasn't
does gynnon ni ddim	we haven't
does gynnoch chi ddim	you haven't (pl)
does ganddyn nhw ddim	they haven't

*The Welsh for "has" or "have" is always **mae gan** when you use a name or names instead of "he", "she" or "they", so you say **mae ganddyn nhw** (they have), but **mae gan Catrin a Rhian** (Catrin and Rhian have).

Talking about your family

On these two pages you will learn lots of words which will help you to talk about your family. You will also find out how to say "my" and "your" and describe people.

Dyma fy nheulu.

fy nghi

fy nhaid

fy nhad

fy chwaer

fy ewythr

fy nghath

fy nain

fy mam

fy mrawd

fy modryb

Who's who?

Dyma dy frawd?

Ie, dyma fy mrawd.

A dyma dy chwaer?

Ie, ei henw ydy Nia.

A dyma dy rieni?

Na, dyma fy nhaid a nain.

New words

teulu	family	**modryb**	aunt	**tenau**	thin
taid	grandfather	**taid a nain**	grandparents	**hen**	old
nain	grandmother	**rhieni**	parents	**ifanc**	young
tad	father	**tal**	tall	**golau**	fair
mam	mother	**bach**	small	**tywyll**	dark-haired
ewythr	uncle	**tew**	fat	**cyfeillgar**	friendly

How to say "my" and "your"

The word for "my" is **fy** and the word for "your" is **dy**. Nouns which begin with the consonant p, t, c, b, d, g, ll, m, or rh change when you use them with **fy** (my) or **dy** (your). These changes are called "mutations". After **fy** there is a "nasal" mutation, e.g. **tad** (father), but **fy nhad** (my father). After **dy**, the mutation is "soft", e.g. **brawd** (brother), but **dy frawd** (your brother).*

*There is a third kind of mutation in Welsh, called "aspirate". You can find out more about this on page 42 where a table of mutations is shown.

Describing your family

Mae fy nhad yn dal ond mae mam yn fach.

Mae fy mam yn dal ond mae dad yn fach.

Mae fy ewythr yn dew ond mae fy modryb yn denau.

Mae taid a nain yn hen ond rydw i yn ifanc.

Mae fy mrawd yn dywyll ond mae fy chwaer yn olau.

Mae fy nghi yn gyfeillgar.

Describing words

In Welsh, you do not say "a big dog" but "dog big": **ci mawr**. The adjective usually comes after the noun. Like some nouns, adjectives can change or "mutate softly" (see box opposite). This happens after **yn**, e.g. **tal** (tall) but **Mae fy nhad yn dal** (My father is tall).*

Try and describe each of these people in Welsh, starting **Mae o/hi yn** (he/she is).

*The change happens to adjectives which start with the consonants listed in the box on page 14. The table of mutations on page 42 shows you what they change to.

Your home

Here you can find out how to say what sort of home you live in and where it is. You can also learn what all the rooms are called.

New words

ble rydych chi'n byw?	where do you live?
mewn tŷ	in a house
fflat	flat
castell	castle
y dref	town
y wlad	country
wrth y môr	by the sea
ysbryd	ghost
ble mae?	where is?
ble mae pawb?	where is everyone?
ystafell ymolchi	bathroom
llofft	upstairs
ystafell wely	bedroom
ystafell fyw	living-room
ystafell fwyta	dining-room
y gegin	kitchen

Where do you live?

Ble rydych chi'n byw?

Rydw i'n byw mewn tŷ.

Rydw i'n byw mewn fflat.

Rydw i'n byw mewn castell.

Town or country?

Rydw i'n byw yn y dref.

Rydw i'n byw yn y wlad.

Rydw i'n byw wrth y môr.

Where is everyone?

Dad comes home and wants to know where everyone is. Look at the pictures and see if you can tell him where everyone is, e.g. **Mae mam** **yn yr ystafell wely**. Look at the box at the bottom of the page, then see if you can answer the questions below the little pictures.

Mam   Dad   Taid

Nain   Rhys   Bethan

Dafydd   ysbryd

Rydw i yn yr ystafell ymolchi.

Rydw i yn y llofft.

Rydw i yn ystafell wely Bethan.

Rydw i yn yr ystafell fyw.

Rydw i yn yr ystafell wely.

Ble mae pawb?

Rydyn ni yn yr ystafell fwyta.

Rydw i yn y gegin.

Pwy sydd yn yr ystafell fyw?

Pwy sydd yn y gegin?

Pwy sydd yn y llofft?

Ble mae Rhys?

Ble mae yr ysbryd?

Ble mae taid?

Points to remember

To answer a question beginning **pwy sydd** (who is), all you have to do is replace **pwy** with the name of the person, e.g. **Pwy sydd yn y gegin** (who is in the kitchen)? **Dafydd sydd yn y gegin** (Dafydd is in the kitchen).

Looking for things

Here you can find out how to ask someone what they are looking for and tell them where things are. You can also learn lots of words for things around the house.

New words

chwilio am	looking for
mochyn-cwta	hamster/guinea pig
beth wyt ti'n ei wneud?	what are you doing?
ar ben	on top of
o dan	under
tu ôl	behind
yn y/mewn	in the/in a
wrth ochr	by the side of
o flaen	in front of
cwpwrdd dillad	wardrobe
soffa	sofa
llenni	curtains
pot blodau	flower pot
silff	shelf
cwpwrdd	cupboard
teledu	television
carped	carpet
cadair-freichiau	armchair
llestr blodau	vase
bwrdd	table
ffôn	telephone

How to say "it"

There isn't a special word for "it" in Welsh. You use "he/him" (**hwn/o**) or "she/her" (**hi/hon**) depending on whether the word you are replacing is masculine or feminine:*

Ble mae'r ffôn (Where is the telephone)?
Mae o ar y bwrdd (It/he is on the table.

Ble mae'r gadair-freichiau (Where is the armchair)?
Mae hi yn yr ystafell fyw (It/she is in the living-room).

The missing hamster

18   *When you are first learning Welsh, it is best not to worry about this, but the Glossary on pages 46-48 tells you if a noun is masculine (m) or feminine (f).

In, on or under?

Try to learn these words by heart. Note the difference between **yn** and **mewn**. **Yn** means "in the", e.g. **yn y bocs** (in the box), **mewn** means "in a", e.g. **mewn bocs** (in a box).

| yn/mewn | tu ôl | o flaen | wrth ochr | o dan | ar ben |

Where are they hiding?

Mr. Owen's six pets are hiding somewhere in the room, but he cannot find them. Can you tell him where they are in Welsh, using the words above?

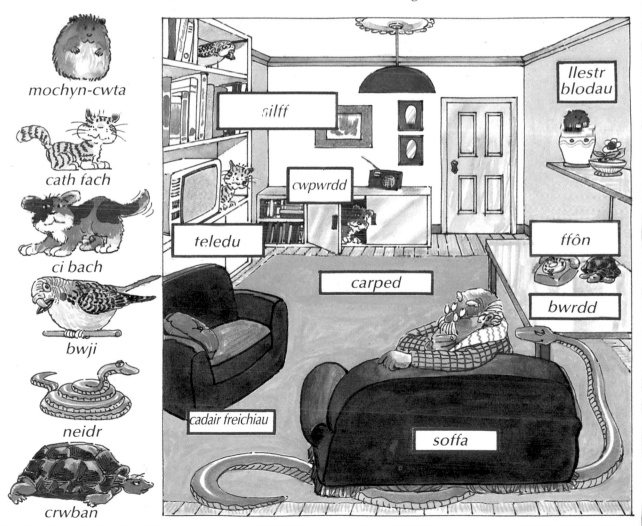

mochyn-cwta

cath fach

ci bach

bwji

neidr

crwban

llestr blodau

silff

cwpwrdd

teledu

carped

ffôn

cadair freichiau

bwrdd

soffa

What do you like eating?

Here you can find out how to say what you like and don't like.

New words

hoffi	to like
ydych chi'n hoffi?	do you like?
pysgod	fish
na dim o gwbl	no, not at all
sglodion	chips
cacen	cake
yn fawr iawn	very much
beth ydych chi yn ei hoffi?	what do you like?
gorau	best/most
selsig	sausage
mae'n well gen i	I prefer
stêc	steak
sbageti	spaghetti
bwyta	eating/ to eat
bara a chaws*	bread and cheese
reis	rice
a finnau hefyd	me too

What do you like?

Ydych chi'n hoffi salad?

Na, dydw i ddim yn hoffi salad.

Ydych chi'n hoffi pysgod?

Na dim o gwbl.

Beth ydych chi yn ei hoffi?

Rydw i'n hoffi sglodion . . .

Rydw i'n hoffi cacen yn fawr iawn.

What do you like best?

Beth ydych chi'n ei hoffi orau?

Rydw i'n hoffi selsig.

Mae'n well gen i stêc.

Ond sbageti rydw i'n hoffi orau.

20   *The word for "cheese" is **caws**, but it mutates (changes) to **chaws** in the phrase "bread and cheese".

What are they eating?

- Beth wyt ti yn ei fwyta?
- Rydw i yn bwyta pitsa.
- Mae hi'n bwyta sglodion.
- Mae o'n bwyta bara a chaws.
- Rydyn ni yn bwyta "hamburger".
- Rydych chi yn bwyta reis.
- Maen nhw yn bwyta banana.

Who likes what?

Who likes cheese? Who doesn't like ham? Who prefers grapes to bananas?

Can you say in Welsh what you like and what you don't like? (See bottom of the page.)

- A finnau hefyd, ond dydw i ddim yn hoffi cig moch
- Rydw i'n hoffi banana.
- Mae'n well gen i rawnwin
- Rydw i'n hoffi caws.
- Rydw i'n hoffi tarten ffrwythau orau.

Jac — Dafydd — Taid — Bethan — Daniel

cig moch — menyn — pastai — bara — tomato — caws — banana — grawnwin — tarten ffrwythau — sudd oren

---

Saying what you like

If someone asks you **Beth ydych chi'n hoffi** (what do you like)?, you begin your answer **Rydw i 'n hoffi** (I like) . . . or **Dydw i ddim yn hoffi** (I don't like) . . . It is also useful to remember how to say "I would like . . .": **Hoffwn i . . .**

21

Table talk

Here you can learn all sorts of useful things to say if you are having a meal with Welsh-speaking friends.

New words

dewch at y bwrdd	come to the table
os gwelwch yn dda	please/yes, please
rydw i eisiau bwyd	I'm hungry
finnau hefyd	me too
helpa dy hun	help yourself
mae'r bwyd yn dda iawn	the food is very good
wyt ti eisiau bwyd?	are you hungry?
pasiwch	pass me
dŵr	water
gwydr	glass
hoffech chi fwy o gig?	would you like some more meat?
cig	meat
dim diolch	no thank you
oedd y bwyd yn dda?	was the food good?
bendigedig	delicious

Dinner is ready

Dewch at y bwrdd os gwelwch yn dda.

Rydw i eisiau bwyd.

A finnau hefyd.

Helpa dy hun.

Diolch yn fawr.

Wyt ti eisiau bwyd?

Ydw, mae'r bwyd yn dda iawn.

Please will you pass me . . .

Pasiwch y dŵr os gwelwch yn dda?

Pasiwch y bara os gwelwch yn dda.

Pasiwch wydr i mi os gwelwch yn dda.

Would you like some more?

Who is saying what?

These little pictures show you different mealtimes. Cover up the rest of the page and see if you know what everyone would say in Welsh.

Bryn is saying he is hungry.

The chef is asking: "Are you hungry?"

Bethan is saying: "Help yourself."

Rhys wants someone to pass him a glass.

Nain is offering Bryn more chips.

He says: "Yes please."

Then he says: "No thanks, I've had enough."

Marc is saying the food is delicious.

The polite word for "you"

There are two words for "you" in Welsh: **ti** and **chi**. You say **ti** to a friend but **chi** to anyone older than you.* **Chi** is more polite and shows you respect the person you are talking to: **ydych chi'n** (are you) . . .? **ydych chi yn** (do you) . . .?

*You can find out more about **ti** and **chi** on page 30.

Your hobbies

These people are talking about their hobbies.

New words

beth wyt ti'n hoffi ei wneud?	what do you like doing?
arlunio	art
coginio	cooking
diddordebau	hobbies
gwneud pethau	making/ doing things
dawnsio	dancing
gyda'r nos	at night
darllen	reading
gwylio'r teledu	watching television
gwau	knitting
beth ydy dy ddiddordebau?	what are your hobbies?
chwaraeon	sport
nofio	swimming
pêl-droed	football
gwrando ar recordiau	listening to records
chwarae offerynnau	playing instruments
ffidil	violin

Saying what you do and what you are doing

Welsh verbs don't have different forms for this: the Welsh for both "I swim" and "I am swimming" is **rydw i yn nofio** (see page 11).

Welsh speakers make clear whether they mean "I can swim" or "I am swimming right now" by the way they say **yn**. In the first case, **yn** is stressed (said clearly and a little louder than the other words). Otherwise the **yn** is not said very clearly, and you will often hardly hear it at all.

> Beth wyt t'in hoffi ei wneud?

> Rydw i'n hoffi arlunio.

> Ond dydw i ddim yn hoffi coginio.

> Beth ydy dy ddiddordebau?

> Rydw i'n hoffi gwneud pethau . . .

> ac yn hoffi dawnsio.

What do you do in the evenings?

> Beth wyt ti'n ei wneud gyda'r nos?

> Rydw i yn darllen . . .

> yn gwylio'r teledu ac yn gwau.

The sporty type

Beth ydy dy ddiddor-debau?

Rydw i yn hoffi chwaraeon.

Rydw i yn nofio . . .

yn chwarae pêl-droed . . .

ac yn chwarae tenis.

Music lovers

Beth wyt ti'n ei hoffi?

Rydw i yn hoffi gwrando ar recordiau.

Ydych chi'n chwarae offerynau?

A rydw i yn chwarae'r piano.

Ydw, rydw i'n chwarae'r ffidil.

What are they doing?

A
B
C
D
E

Cover up the rest of the page and see if you can say in Welsh what all these people are doing, e.g. **mae o yn** or **mae hi yn . . .**
Can you say in Welsh what your hobbies are?

25

Telling the time

Here you can find out how to tell the time in Welsh.

You can look up numbers on page 40. There is a special way of saying 20 and 25 when you are telling the time: 20 is **ugain munud** and 25 is **pum munud ar again.** The word for "past" is **wedi** and the word for "to" is **i.**

What is the time?

Here is how to ask what the time is.

New words

faint o'r gloch ydy hi?	what time is it?
mae hi'n . . .	it is . . .
un o'r gloch	one o' clock
saith o'r gloch	seven o' clock
pum munud wedi	five past
chwarter wedi	quarter past
hanner awr wedi*	half past
chwarter i	quarter to
pum munud i	five to
hanner nos*	midnight
hanner dydd*	midday
yn y bore	in the morning
yn yr hwyr	in the evening
codi	to get up
ysgol	school
chwarae pêl-droed	to play football
gwylio'r teledu	watching television
i'r gwely	to bed

Mealtimes

brecwast	breakfast
cinio	dinner
te	tea
swper	supper

The time is . . .

Mae hi'n bum munud wedi naw.

Mae hi'n chwarter wedi naw.

Mae hi'n hanner awr wedi naw.

Mae hi'n chwarter i ddeg.

Mae hi'n bum munud i ddeg.

Mae hi'n hanner nos/hanner dydd.

What time of day?

Mae hi'n chwech o'r gloch yn y bore.

Mae hi'n chwech o'r gloch yn yr hwyr.

26   *To say "half past twelve" you say **hanner awr wedi hanner dydd/hanner nos**.

Marc's day

Read what Marc does throughout the day, then see if you can match each clock with the right picture. You can find out what the answers are on pages 44-45.

 a
 b
 c
 d
 e
 f
 g
 h

1 Mae Marc yn codi am hanner awr wedi saith.

2 Mae o'n bwyta brecwast am wyth o'r gloch.

3 Mae o'n mynd i'r ysgol am chwarter i i naw.

4 Mae o'n bwyta cinio am hanner awr wedi hanner dydd.

5 Mae o'n chwarae pêl droed am ddeg munud wedi dau.

6 Mae o'n gwylio'r teledu am chwarter wedi pump.

7 Mae o'n cael te am chwech o'r gloch.

8 Mae o'n mynd i'r gwely am hanner awr wedi wyth.

What time is it?

Can you say in Welsh what times these clocks show?

Arranging things

Here is how to arrange things with your friends.

New words

hoffet ti ddod i?	would you like to come to?
pryd?	when?
iawn	all right
tua	about
pwll nofio	swimming pool
yn y prynhawn	in the afternoon
tan	until
heno	tonight
fedra i ddim	I can't
yfory	tomorrow
fe welai di nos yfory	I'll see you tomorrow night
parti	party
rydw i'n mynd i ddawns	I'm going to a dance

Days of the week

Dydd* Llun	Monday
Dydd Mawrth	Tuesday
Dydd Mercher	Wednesday
Dydd Iau	Thursday
Dydd Gwener	Friday
Dydd Sadwrn	Saturday
Dydd Sul	Sunday

Tennis

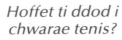

Swimming

Going to the cinema

28   ***Dydd** means "day". Sometimes it is not used when saying "Monday", "Tuesday" etc., e.g. in a diary you might see **Llun, Mawrth . . .**, and "Saturday night" is just **nos Sadwrn**.

Going to a party

Your diary for the week

Here is your diary showing you what you are doing for a week. Read it and see if you can understand what you are doing every day. You can check on pages 44-45.

Llun
4 o'r gloch. Tenis

Mawrth
2 o'r gloch. Piano
5.30 Pwll nofio

Mercher
3 o'r gloch. Tenis
7.45 Sinema

Iau

Gwener
8 o'r gloch. Dawnsio efo Gareth

Sadwrn
2 o'r gloch. pêl-droed
7 o'r gloch. Parti!

Sul
Tenis yn y prynhawn.

Would you like . . .?

In Welsh, when you ask a friend "Would you like . . .?", you say **hoffet ti . . .?** e.g. **Hoffet ti ddod i'r pwll nofio** (Would you like to come to the swimming pool)? It is also useful to learn the **chi** or polite form for this: **hoffech chi** (would you like) . . .? e.g. **Hoffech chi ddod i'r pwll nofio?***

*You can find out more about the difference between **ti** and **chi** on pages 23 and 30.

Asking where places are

Here and on the next two pages you can find out how to ask your way around.

In Welsh there are two words for "you" – **ti** and **chi***. You say **ti** to a friend, but it is more polite to say **chi** when you talk to someone you don't know well or to someone older.

New words

esgusodwch fi	excuse me
diolch yn fawr	thank you very much
croeso	you're welcome
ble mae'r?	where is?
Swyddfa Post	post office
yn y fan acw	over there
drws nesaf	next door
farchnad	market
Gwesty'r Castell	Castle Hotel
trowch	turn
oes caffi'n agos?	is there a café nearby?
Stryd y Castell	Castle Street
ydy o'n bell?	is it far?
nac ydy	no, it's not
ar gornel y stryd	on the street corner
archfarchnad	supermarket
stryd fawr	high street
fferyllydd	chemist

Being polite

This is how to say "Excuse me".

When people thank you, it is polite to answer **Croeso**.

Where is . . .?

Directions

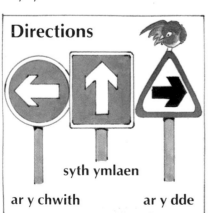

syth ymlaen

ar y chwith   ar y dde

*E.g. the polite form for "How are you?" is **Sut ydych chi?** Remember that in the plural (when you are talking to more than one person), the word for "you" is always **chi**.

Is there a . . . nearby?

Is it far?

Esgusodwch fi, oes caffi yn agos?

Oes mae un yn Stryd y Castell.

Ydy o'n bell?

Nac ydy, trowch i'r dde ar gornel y stryd.

Esgusodwch fi, oes archfarchnad yn agos?

Oes, dros y ffordd yn y stryd fawr.

Ac oes fferyllydd yn agos?

Oes, drws nesaf i'r archfarchnad.

Other useful places to ask for

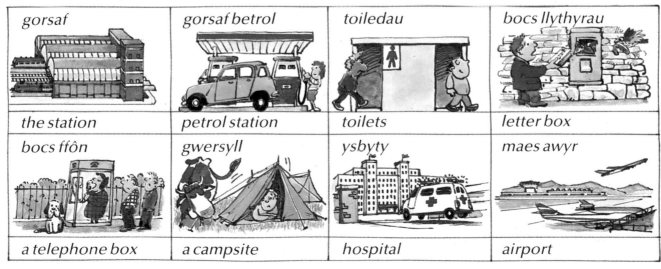

gorsaf	gorsaf betrol	toiledau	bocs llythyrau
the station	petrol station	toilets	letter box
bocs ffôn	gwersyll	ysbyty	maes awyr
a telephone box	a campsite	hospital	airport

Finding your way around

Here you can find out how to ask your way around and follow directions. When you have read everything, try the map puzzle on the opposite page.

Ble mae'r orsaf os gwelwch yn dda?*

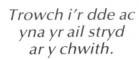

Trowch i'r dde ac yna yr ail stryd ar y chwith.

Mae'r orsaf ar y dde.

Ble mae'r hostel ieuenctid os gwelwch yn dda.

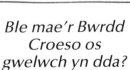

Ewch yn syth ymlaen ac yna y trydydd stryd ar y dde.

Mae'r hostel ar y chwith.

Ble mae'r Bwrdd Croeso os gwelwch yn dda?

Yn y car? Ewch yn syth ymlaen . . .

a trowch i lawr y stryd gyntaf ar y chwith.

Os gwelwch yn dda is the polite way to say "please".

New words

ble mae'r?	where is?	**y stryd gyntaf**	first street
yr ail stryd	the second street	**eglwys**	church
hostel ieuenctid	youth hostel	**ysgol**	school
ac yna	and then	**neuadd y dref**	town hall
trydydd	third	**siopau**	shops
Bwrdd Croeso	Tourist Board	**pwll nofio**	swimming pool
yn y car	in the car		

Telling people what to do

In Welsh, to tell people which way to go or what to do, you usually drop the last letter of the verb and add **wch**, e.g. **troi** (to turn) changes to **trowch** (turn).

Some useful commands that do not follow this pattern are: **Ewch!** (go); **dewch yma!** (come here); **cymerwch!** (take).

Finding your way around Llanbrynybugailmwyn

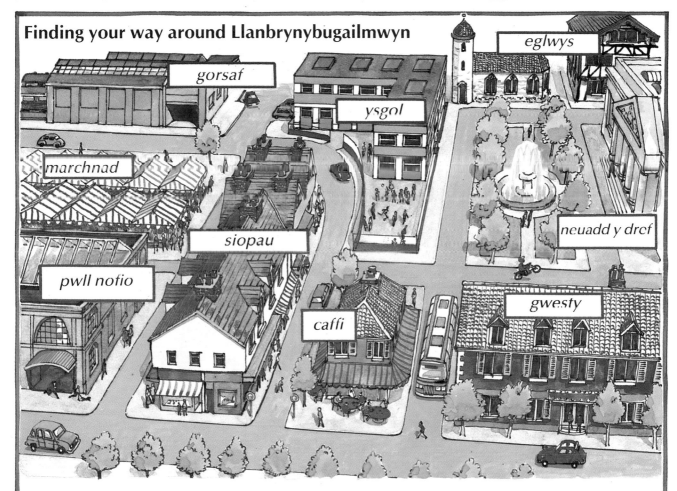

How would you ask someone the way to the market place?
How would you ask them if there is a café nearby?

Can you tell the person in the yellow car how to get to the school?
Can you direct someone from the hotel to the market?

Going shopping

Here and on the next two pages you can find out how to say what you want when you go shopping.

Money in Welsh

The Welsh **ceiniog** and **punt** are worth the same as the penny and the pound. Numbers are listed on page 40.

New words

mynd i	going
siopa	shopping
prynu	to buy
siop fara	baker's
groser	grocer
llefrith	milk
wy(au)	egg(s)
ffrwythau	fruit
llysiau	vegetables
cigydd	butcher
cig	meat
hanner	half a
dwsin	dozen
o'er rhain	of these
rhywbeth arall?	anything else?
ceiniog	penny/pence
punt	pound (s)
pwys	pound (weight)
afal(au)	apple(s)
hanner pwys	half a pound

Plural nouns

The words **ceiniog** and **punt** do not change whether you are talking about one or many. Quite a few nouns add "au" to form the plural, e.g. **wy** (egg), but **wyau** (eggs), but many nouns change in other ways, e.g. **aderyn** (bird), but **adar** (birds). The Glossary on pages 46-8 shows you both the singular and plural forms.

Mrs. Jones goes shopping

Mae Mrs. Jones yn mynd i siopa.

Mae hi'n prynu bara yn y siop fara.

Yn y siop fara

Bore da.

Bore da Mrs. Jones.

Hanner dwsin o'r rhain os gwelwch yn dda.

Rhwybeth arall?

Trideg ceiniog os gwelwch yn dda.

Dim diolch.

Diolch yn fawr.

Mae hi'n prynu llefrith ac wyau yn siop y groser.

Mae hi'n prynu ffrwythau a llysiau yn y farchnad.

Mae hi'n prynu cig yn siop y cigydd.

Yn siop y groser

Beth hof-fech chi?

Hanner dwsin o wyau os gwelwch yn dda.

Rhywbeth arall?

Peint o lctrith os gwelwch yn dda.

Diolch yn fawr.

Wythdeg pump ceiniog os gwelwch yn dda.

85c

Yn y farchnad

Bore da Mrs. Jones, beth hoffech chi?

Pwys o afalau os gwelwch yn dda.

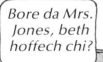

Rhyw-beth arall?

Hanner pwys o domatos.

Chwedeg pump ceiniog os gwelwch yn dda.

65c

More shopping and going to a café

Here you can find out how to ask how much things cost and how to order things in a café.

New words

faint ydy?	how much?
cardiau post	postcards
yr un	each
y pwys	a pound
rhosyn	rose
fe gymera i	I will have/take
cwpaned o goffi	cup of coffee
dyma'r coffi	here is the coffee
afal (au)	apple(s)
pînafal	pineapple
lemwn	lemon
oren(nau)	orange(s)
eirin gwlanog	peaches
grawnwin	grapes
lemonêd	lemonade
tê hefo llefrith	tea with milk
hefo lemwn	with lemon
sudd oren	orange juice
siocled poeth	hot chocolate
hufen iâ	ice-cream

Asking how much things cost

Faint ydy'r cardiau post?

Deg ceiniog yr un.

Faint ydy'r grawnwin?

Chwedeg ceiniog y pwys.

60c

Faint ydy un rhosyn?

Pumdeg ceiniog.

Fe gymera i saith os gwelwch yn dda.

50c

Going to a café

Beth hoffech chi?

Cwpaned o goffi os gwelwch yn dda.

Dyma'r coffi.

Diolch.

Faint ydy'r coffi?

Trideg ceiniog os gwelwch yn dda.

Buying fruit

Everything on the fruit stall is marked with its name and price.

Look at the picture, then see if you can answer the questions below.

AFALAU
30c
y pwys

Beth
hoffech chi?

BANANA
40c
y pwys

GRAWNWIN
60c
y pwys

ORENNAU
30c
yr un

PÎNAFAL
80c
yr un

EIRIN
GWLANOG
90c y pwys

LEMWN
15c
yr un

How do you tell the stallholder you would like four lemons, a pound of bananas and a pineapple? How much do each of these things cost?

Faint ydy'r afalau y pwys?
Faint ydy pînafal yr un?
Faint ydy'r eirin gwlanog y pwys?
Faint ydy un lemwn a phwys o afalau?

Things to order

Here are some things you might want to order in a café.

Rydw i eisiau . . .

lemonêd	cola	tê hefo llefrith	tê hefo lemwn
sudd	siocled poeth	llefrith	hufen-iâ

The months and seasons

Here you can learn what the seasons and months are called and find out how to say what the date is.

New words

mis	month
blwyddyn	year
heddiw	today
dyddiad	date
penblwydd	birthday

The seasons

gwanwyn	spring
haf	summer
hydref	autumn
gaeaf	winter

The months

Ionawr	January
Chwefror	February
Mawrth	March
Ebrill	April
Mai	May
Mehefin	June
Gorffenaf	July
Awst	August
Medi	September
Hydref	October
Tachwedd	November
Rhagfyr	December

The seasons

gwanwyn

Mawrth, Ebrill, Mai . . .

haf

Mehefin, Gorffenaf, Awst . . .

hydref

Medi, Hydref, Tachwedd . . .

gaeaf

Rhagfyr, Ionawr, Chwefror.

How to say "first", "second", "third" . . .

cyntaf	first
ail	second
trydydd	third
pedwerydd	fourth
pumed	fifth
chweched	sixth
seithfed	seventh
wythfed	eighth
nawfed	ninth
degfed	tenth

Ionawr ydy'r mis cyntaf yn y flwyddyn.

Awst, ydy'r wythfed mis yn y flwyddyn.

Chwefror ydy'r ail fis yn y flwyddyn.

Can you say where the rest of the months come in the year?

What is the date?

Heddiw ydy'r trydydd o Fai.

Beth ydy'r dyddiad heddiw?

Y cyntaf o Ionawr.

Writing the date

Bangor
y 1af o Fai

Here you can see how a date is written. You put **y**, the number, **o** (of) and the month.* For "the first" you put **y 1af**.

When is your birthday?

Pryd mae dy benblwydd?

Ar y degfed o fis Tachwedd.

Mae fy mhenblwydd i ar Chwefror undeg dau.

Mae penblwydd Wil ar yr wythfed o Fehefin.

When are their birthdays?

The dates of the children's birthdays are written below their pictures. See if you can say in Welsh when they are, e.g. **Mae penblwydd Nia ar yr ail o Ebrill.**

Nia	*Selwyn*	*Elin*	*Mari*	*Aled*	*Dewi*

2 o Ebrill	*21 o Fehefin*	*18 o Hydref*	*6 o Awst*	*13 o Fawrth*	*7 o Fedi*

*The month also takes a soft mutation, e.g. **Mai** (May) but **o Fai** (of May).

39

Colours and numbers

Colours are describing words (adjectives), so in Welsh they come after the word they refer to, e.g. **gwallt du** (black hair).

The colours*

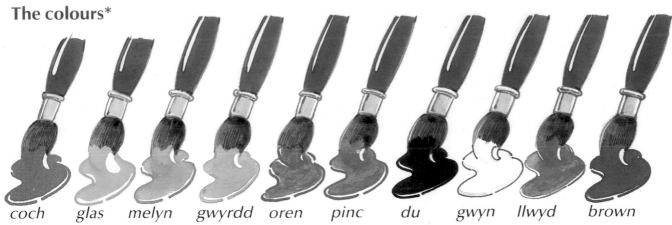

coch   glas   melyn   gwyrdd   oren   pinc   du   gwyn   llwyd   brown

What colour is it?

Cover the picture above and see if you can say what colour everything is in the painting. You should know all the words you need.

Numbers

You count the 30s, 40s, 50s, 60s, 70s, 80s and 90s in the same way as 20-29.

1 un	11 undeg un	21 dauddeg un	40 pedwardeg
2 dau/dwy**	12 undeg dau	22 dauddeg dau	50 pumdeg
3 tri/tair	13 undeg tri	23 dauddeg tri	60 chwedeg
4 pedwar/pedair	14 undeg pedwar	24 dauddeg pedwar	70 saithdeg
5 pump	15 undeg pump	25 dauddeg pump	80 wythdeg
6 chwech	16 undeg chwech	26 dauddeg chwech	90 nawdeg
7 saith	17 undeg saith	27 dauddeg saith	100 cant
8 wyth	18 undeg wyth	28 dauddeg wyth	
9 naw	19 undeg naw	29 dauddeg naw	
10 deg	20 dauddeg	30 trideg	

*Colours take a soft mutation after "is" or "are": **yn.** See page 42. **The numbers 2, 3 and 4 have a masculine and a feminine form depending on whether you use them with an (m) or (f) noun.

Pronunciation guide

In Welsh, many letters are not pronounced in the same way as in English. Remember that the Welsh alphabet is a little different (see page 7).

Here is a list of vowels and consonants with a guide to how to say each one. For each Welsh sound, we have shown an English word which sounds like it. Read it out loud in a normal way to find out how to pronounce the Welsh sound.

Welsh vowels

Vowels can be either short or long, so you say:

a   either as in "cat" or as in "card"

e   either as in "ten" or as in "fair"

i   either as in "ink" or as in "mean"

o   either as in "crop" or as in "more"

u   either as in "pin" or as in "been"

w   either as in "took" or as in "moon"

y   either as in "pin" or as in "been"

(Note that "u" and "y" are said in the same way.)

There are hardly any easy rules to help you learn when a vowel is long and when it is short. For example, "e" is short in **pen** (head), but long in **ceg** (mouth). One useful rule you can remember, though, is that the "little roof" always makes a vowel long, e.g. **tŷ**.

When you are not sure, the best thing is to use the short vowel. As long as you get the sound of the consonants right, Welsh people will be able to understand you. In fact, Welsh speakers from different parts of Wales pronounce some vowels differently themselves.

Welsh consonants

Each consonant always has the same sound in Welsh. You say:

b   as in "balloon"

c   as in "cat"

ch   as in the Scottish word "loch"

d   as in "dog"

dd   as in "the" or "soothe"

f   as in "have" (like an English "v")

ff   as in "face" (like an English "f")

g   as in "goal"

ng   as in "long"

h   as in "have"

l   as in "low"

ll   like an "l" but you blow air out at the same time

m   as in "man"

n   as in "name"

p   as in "pen"

ph   as in "friend" (also like an English "f")

r   as in "robin"

rh   like an "r" followed by a "huh" sound

s   as in "sea"

t   as in "table"

th   as in "thick" or "thin"

Grammar

Grammar is like a set of rules about how you put words together and it is different for every language. You will find Welsh easier if you learn some of its grammar, but don't worry if you don't understand it all straight away. Just read a little about it at a time. This is a guide to the grammar used in this book.

Mutations

In Welsh, words which begin with certain consonants sometimes change their first letters. These changes are called mutations.*

The consonants which change are p, t, c, b, d, g, ll, m and rh. Each of these can change in three ways, as there are three kinds of mutation.

The soft mutation is when the consonant changes to a softer sounding one, (e.g. p becomes b) or disappears.

The nasal mutation is when the consonant sounds as if you are holding your nose, e.g. p becomes mh.

The aspirate mutation is when an h follows the first consonant, e.g. p changes to ph.

How mutations happen

Mutations can happen for many different reasons in Welsh, so this book explains just a few important ones.

Nouns always mutate after **fy**, **dy** and **ei** ("my", "your" and "his/her" – see pages 6, 14 and the table below). Feminine singular nouns mutate softly after **y** or **yr** ("the" – see page 43).

Adjectives mutate softly after **yn** (see page 15). They also mutate softly after a feminine noun, e.g. **bach** becomes **fach**: **cath fach** (small cat).

Don't worry if you don't know enough about mutations to remember to change the words whenever you should. Just knowing that they happen helps to spot words which have changed.

Table of mutations

The table below shows you the different changes for each consonant (*in italic letters*). It also shows the mutations which happen with **fy** (my), **dy** (your) and **ei** (his/her).

Consonant	Soft mutation	Nasal mutation	Aspirate mutation
p pen (head)	dy *b*en (your head) ei *b*en (his head)	fy *mh*en (my head)	ei *ph*en (her head)
t tomato (tomato)	dy *d*omato (your tomato) ei *d*omato (his tomato)	fy *nh*omato (my tomato)	ei *th*omato (her tomato)
c ceg (mouth)	dy *g*eg (your mouth) ei *g*eg (his mouth)	fy *ngh*eg (my mouth)	ei *ch*eg (her mouth)
b braich (arm)	dy *f*raich (your arm) ei *f*raich (his arm)	fy *m*raich (my arm)	no mutation
d dant (tooth)	dy *dd*ant (your tooth) ei *dd*ant (his tooth)	fy *n*ant (my tooth)	no mutation
g gardd (garden)	dy *ardd* (your garden) ei *ardd* (his garden)	fy *ng*ardd (my garden)	no mutation
ll llygad (eye)	dy *l*ygad (your eye) ei *l*ygad (his eye)	no mutation	no mutation
m mam (mother)	dy *f*am (your mother) ei *f*am (his mother)	no mutation	no mutation
rh rhaw (spade)	dy *r*aw (your spade) ei *r*aw (his spade)	no mutation	no mutation

*Mutations also happen in English, e.g. when the word "knife" changes to "knives".

Nouns: "a", "an", "the"

There is no word for "a" or "an" in Welsh. To say "a bird", you just say "bird":

aderyn a bird

The word for "the" is **yr** before nouns beginning with a vowel and **y** before nouns beginning with a consonant:

yr aderyn the bird
y ci the dog

Yr often shortens to **'r**: you don't say **a yr** or **ac yr** (and the), but **a'r**:

Y ci a'r gath the cat and the dog

In the same way, **i'r** means "to the" and **o'r** means "from the".

Words which end in a vowel add **'r** instead of being followed by **y** or **yr**:

dyma'r . . . here is the . . .

Masculine and feminine nouns

Welsh nouns are either masculine or feminine. The gender of each noun is shown in the Glossary (pages 46-48).

Feminine singular nouns mutate softly after **y** or **yr** (the), e.g. **cadair** (chair) changes to **y gadair** (the chair). It is best not to worry about this now. (Note that most of the nouns in this book are masculine.)

Plural nouns

In English, most nouns add an "s" in the plural (e.g. dogs). In Welsh, some nouns add "au", but many have different plurals which you have to learn one by one (plurals are shown in the Glossary):

afal, afalau apple, apples

cath, cathod cat, cats

Adjectives

In Welsh, adjectives come after the noun: you say "a dog small": **ci bach.**
Mutation of adjectives is explained on page 42.

"My", "your", "his" and "her"

Fy (my), **dy** (your) and **ei** (his/her) mutate the word used with them: **dy** and **ei** (his) take a soft mutation, **fy** a nasal mutation and **ei** (her) an aspirate mutation. See the table on page 42.

Pronouns

Here are the words for "I", "you" etc.: **i** (I); **ti** (you); **o** (he); **hi** (she); **ni** (we); **chi** (you, plural/polite); **nhw** (they).

Notice how the Welsh word for "I" is **i** (it is not written with a capital letter).

Remember that **ti** (you) is how you address a friend. You say **chi** (you) when you are talking to many people (plural), to someone older than you or to someone you don't know well (polite singular). In Welsh, "it" is **o** (he) or **hi** (she) depending on whether the noun it replaces is masculine or feminine (see page 18).

Verbs

The Welsh verb **bod** (to be) is used to form other verbs:

rydw i	I am
rwyt ti	you are
mae o/hi	he/she/it is
rydyn ni	we are
rydych chi	you are (pol/pl)
maen nhw	they are

You make other verbs with **rydw i** or **rwyt ti** etc. + **yn** + the verb-noun. (The verb-noun is the basic part of a Welsh verb, e.g. **nofio**, which means both "to swim" and "swimming".)

rydw i yn nofio I swim/am swimming

Yn is often shortened to **'n** (see page 11).

Negative verbs: "I am not . . ."

The negative form of **bod** (not to be) is used to form other negative verbs:

dydw i ddim	I am not
dwyt ti ddim	you are not
dydy o/hi ddim	he/she/it is not
dydyn ni ddim	we are not
dydych chi ddim	you are not (pol/pl)
dydyn nhw ddim	they are not

You make other negative verbs with **dydw i ddim** or **dwyt ti ddim** etc. + **yn** + the verb-noun:

dydw i ddim yn nofio I am not swimming/don't swim
dwyt ti ddim yn nofio you are not swimming/don't swim

Answers to puzzles

p.5

How are you?

Yn wael/Yn ofnadwy.
Dim yn dda.
Yn weddol.
Yn dda.
Yn dda iawn.

p.7

What are they called?

Ei enw o ydy Rhys.
Ei henw hi ydy Mari.
Eu henwau nhw ydy Ann a Gary.
Fy enw i ydy . . . (or) . . . ydw i.

Who is who?

John is talking to Sian.
Sian is talking to Carys.
Gwilym is reading the paper in the pool.
The man talking to him is lying by the pool.
John is wearing the green bathing cap.

p.9

Can you remember?

Blodyn, cath, coeden, nyth, aderyn, tŷ, haul,
ffenestr, car, ci.

p.11

Who comes from where?

Franz comes from Austria.
The French contestants are called Pierre and
Marie.
Lolita is Spanish.
Yes, there is a Scottish contestant.
Marie and Pierre are from France.
Yuri comes from Moscow. Moscow is in
Russia.

p.13

How old are they?

Maldwyn is nearly fourteen.
Catrin and Rhian are fifteen.

Griff is thirteen.
Gwen is eleven.
Iwan is nine.
Nerys is six.

How many brothers and sisters?

Catrin a Rhian = A
Gwen = E
Maldwyn = C
Iwan = B
Griff = D

p.17

Where is everyone?

Nain sydd yn yr ystafell fyw.
Dafydd sydd yn y gegin.
Bethan sydd yn y llofft.
Mae Rhys yn yr ystafell ymolchi.
Mae'r ysbryd yn ystafell wely Bethan.
Mae taid yn yr ystafell fwyta.

p.19

Where are they hiding?

Mae'r mochyn-cwta yn y llestr blodau.
Mae'r gath fach tu ôl y teledu.
Mae'r ci bach yn y cwpwrdd.
Mae'r bwji ar ben y silff.
Mae'r neidr o flaen y soffa.
Mae'r crwban wrth ochr y ffôn.

p.21

Who likes what?

Daniel likes cheese.
Jac doesn't like ham.
Taid prefers grapes to bananas.

p.23

Who is saying what?

"Rydw i eisiau bwyd."
"Wyt ti eisiau bwyd?"/"Ydych chi eisiau bwyd?"
"Helpa dy hun".
"Pasiwch wydr i mi so gwelwch yn dda".

"Hoffech chi fwy o sglodion?".
"Os gwelwch yn dda."
"Dim diolch, rydw i wedi cael digon".
"Bendigedig".

p.25

What are they doing?

A Mae o yn coginio.
B Mae o yn nofio.
C Maen nhw yn dawnsio.
D Mae hi yn chwarae'r ffidil.
E Mae o yn arlunio.

p.27

Marc's day

a 4, b 1, c 8, d 7, e 2, f 3, g 6, h 5.

What time is it?

a Pum munud wedi tri.
b Pum munud wedi unarddeg.
c Deg munud i naw.
d Chwarter i bedwar.
e Pum munud ar ugain wedi tri.
f Hanner awr wedi saith.
g Tri o'r gloch.
h Pedwar o'r gloch.
i Naw o'r gloch.
j Hanner awr wedi un.
k Pum munud wedi saith.
l Hanner awr wedi deg.
m Chwech o'r gloch.
n Pum munud ar ugain i bedwar.
o Pum munud i ddau.

p.29

Your diary for the week

Monday:	4 o'clock	Tennis
Tuesday:	2 o'clock	Piano
	5.30	Swimming pool
Wednesday:	3 o'clock	Tennis
	7.45	Cinema
Thursday:	no plans	
Friday:	Dancing with Gareth	
Saturday:	2 o'clock	Football
	7 o'clock	Party
Sunday:	Tennis in the afternoon	

p.33

Finding your way around

Ble mae'r farchnad os gwelwch yn dda?
Oes caffi yn agos?
Trowch i'r chwith ac ewch yn syth ymlaen.
Trowch i'r dde yn ymyl y pwll nofio, yna ewch yn syth ymlaen.

p.37

Buying fruit

Pedwar lemwn, pwys o fananas a pînafal os gwelwch yn dda.
Lemon: 15p each.
Bananas: 40p per pound.
Pineapple: 80p each.
Mae'r afalau yn 30c y pwys.
Mae'r pînafal yn 80c yr un.
Mae'r eirin gwlanog yn 90c y pwys.
Maen nhw yn 4'ir

p.39

When are their birthdays?

Nia: Ail o Ebrill.
Selwyn: Mehefin dauddeg un.
Elin: Hydref undegwyth.
Mari: Chweched o Awst.
Aled: Mawrth undegtri.
Dewi: Seithfed o Fedi.

p.40

What colour is it?

Mae'r haul yn felyn.
Mae'r tô yn oren.
Mae'r awyr yn las.
Mae'r blodau yn binc.
Mae'r ci yn frown.
Mae'r aderyn yn ddu.
Mae'r car yn goch.
Mae'r goeden yn wyrdd.
Mae'r tŷ yn wyn.

Glossary

Each noun is followed by its plural form in brackets, then (m) or (f) to show if it is masculine or feminine.* If you cannot find a word, remember it may have changed its beginning (it may have mutated), and you should look for it under a different letter (see the table of mutations on page 42).

A

a/ac	and
aderyn (adar) (m)	bird
afal (afalau) (m)	apple
Almaen	Germany
ar ben	on top of
archfarchnad	supermarket
arlunio	art, painting
Awst	August
Awstria	Austria

B

bach	small
banana (bananas) (m)	banana
banc (banciau) (m)	bank
bara (m)	bread
beth?	what?
ble mae?	where is?
blodyn (blodau) (m)	flower
blwyddyn (blynyddoedd) (f)	year
bocs (bocsiau) (m)	box
bocs llythyrau	letter box
bore (boreau) (m)	morning
brawd (brodyr) (m)	brother
brecwast	breakfast
brown	brown
bwrdd (byrddau) (m)	table
bwyta	to eat
byw	to live

C

cacen (cacennau) (f)	cake
cadair (cadeiriau) (f)	chair
caffi (m)	café
Canolfan Croeso	Tourist Office
Canolfan Ieuenctid	Youth Hostel
car (ceir) (m)	car
carped (carpedi) (m)	carpet
cath (cathod) (f)	cat
caws (m)	cheese
ci (cŵn) (m)	dog
cig moch (m)	bacon, ham
cinio (m)	dinner
coch	red
codi	to get up
coeden (coed) (f)	tree
coffi (m)	coffee
coginio	to cook
croeso	you're welcome

crwban (m)	tortoise
cwpan (cwpannau) (f)	cup
cwpwrdd (cypyrddau) (m)	cupboard
cwpaned	cup of
cyfeillgar	friendly
Cymraeg	Welsh
Cymru	Wales

CH

chwaer (chwiorydd) (f)	sister
chwarae	to play
chwaraeon	games
Chwefror	February
chwith	left

D

da	good
da boch	goodbye
darllen	to read
dawnsio	to dance
dewch!	come!
diddordeb (diddorbebau) (m)	interest
digon	enough
diolch	thank you
dipyn bach	a little
dod	to come
dod o	to come from
drws (drysau) (m)	door
dy	your
dydd (diwrnod) (m)	day
dyddiad (m)	date
dyma	here is, this is
dyna	that is

E

Ebrill	April
eglwys (eglwysi) (f)	church
ei	his, her
eisiau	to want
eirin gwlanog (f)	peaches
enw (enwau) (m)	name
esgusodwch fi	excuse me
eu	their
ewythr (ewythredd) (m)	uncle

F

faint?	how much?
faint o'r gloch?	what time is it?
finnau hefyd	me too
fy	my

*Plural forms of nouns are left out if they are not useful. Nouns which are generally used in the plural are given only in the plural in both Welsh and English.

FF

ffenestr (ffenestri) (f)	window
fferyllydd (m)	chemist
ffidil (m)	violin
ffôn (m)	telephone
Ffrainc	France
Ffrangeg	French
ffrind (ffrindiau) (m/f)	friend

G

gaeaf	winter
ga'i	can I have
garej (m)	garage
gegin (f)	kitchen
glas	blue
golau	fair, light
Gorffenaf	July
gorsaf (gorsafoedd) (f)	station
gorsaf betrol (f)	petrol station
grawnwin	grapes
gwael	poor, poorly
gwallt (m)	hair
gwanwyn	spring
gwau	knitting
gweddol	fair
(Dydd) Gwener	Friday
gwely (gwelyau) (m)	bed
gwesty (m)	hotel
gwlad (gwledydd) (f)	country
gwneud pethau	to make things
gwrando	to listen
gwydr (gwydrau) (m)	glass
gwyn	white
gwylio	to watch
gyda'r nos	at night, evening

H

haf	summer
helo	hello
helpa dy hun	help yourself
hen	old
mhoff	favourite
hoffi	to like
hon	she, her
hwn	him, he
hwyl fawr	goodbye
(yr) hwyr	late evening
Hydref	October, autumn

I

(Dydd) Iau	Thursday
iawn	very, right
ifanc	young
Ionawr	January

L

lemonêd (m)	lemonade
lemwn (m)	lemon

LL

llefrith (m)	milk
llestr blodau (m)	vase
Lloegr	England
(Dydd) Llun	Monday
llun (lluniau) (m)	picture
llwyd	grey

M

Mai	May
Medi	September
melyn	yellow
menyn (m)	butter
(Dydd) Mercher	Wednesday
mis (misoedd) (m)	month
mewn	in a
mochyn-cwta (m)	hamster, guinea pig
modryb (modrybedd) (f)	aunt

N

na	no
nac ydw	no, I'm not
nain (neiniau) (f)	grandmother
neidr (nadroedd) (f)	snake
Neuadd y Dref	Town Hall
nhw	them, they
nofio	to swim, swimming
nos (m)	night
noswaith (f)	evening

O

o	from
o dan	under
oed	age
offeryn (offerynau) (m)	musical instrument
o flaen	in front of
ond	but
oren (orennau) (m)	orange

P

parti (partion) (m)	party
pastai (m)	pie
pêl-droed (f)	football
penblwydd	birthday
piano (m)	piano
pînafal (m)	pineapple
pinc	pink
pitsa (m)	pizza
pryd?	when?
prynhawn	afternoon
pwll nofio (m)	swimming-pool
pysgodyn (pysgod) (m)	fish

R

reis (m)	rice
Rwsia	Russia

RH

Rhagfyr	December
rhieni	parents
rhosyn (rhosod) (m)	rose

S

(Dydd) Sadwrn	Saturday
Saesneg	English
salad (m)	salad
Sbaen	Spain
sbageti (m)	spaghetti
selsig (m)	sausage
sglodion	chips
siarad	to talk, speak
simne (simneau) (m)	chimney
sinema (m)	cinema
siop y cigydd	butcher's
siop fara	baker's
siop y groser	grocer's
soffa (f)	sofa
stêc (m)	steak
sudd oren (m)	orange juice
(Dydd) Sul	Sunday
sut?	how?
syth ymlaen	straight ahead

T

Tachwedd	November
tad (tadau) (m)	father
taid (teidiau) (m)	grandfather
tal	tall
tarten ffrwythau (f)	fruit tart
te (m)	tea
teledu (m)	television
tenau	thin
tenis	tennis
teulu (teuluoedd) (m)	family
tô (m)	roof
toiled (toiledau) (m)	toilet
tomato (m)	tomato
tref (trefi) (f)	town
tu ôl	behind
tŷ (tai) (m)	house
tywyll	dark-haired

W

wrth ochr	by the side of
wrth ymyl	near to
wŷ (wyau) (m)	egg

Y

y/yr	the
y dde	the right
yfory	tomorrow
yn fawr iawn	very much
ysbyty (ysbytai) (f)	hospital
ysgol (ysgolion) (f)	school
ystafell fwyta (f)	dining-room
ystafell fyw (f)	living-room
ystafell molchi (m)	bathroom
ystafell wely (f)	bedroom

First published in 1989 by Usborne Publishing Ltd.
Usborne House, 83-85 Saffron Hill
London EC1N 8RT, England.

Copyright © 1989 Usborne Publishing Ltd.

Printed in Great Britain.